THE TAOS CRESCENT

THE TAOS CRESCENT

PHILLIPS KLOSS

Sunstone Press
Santa Fe, New Mexico

FIRST EDITION

Printed in the United States of America

Library of Congress Cataloging in Publication Data:

Kloss, Phillips Wray, 1902-
    The Taos crescent / Phillips Kloss. -- 1st ed.
       p. cm.
      ISBN 0-86534-165-6 (hardcover)   ISBN 978-1-63293-150-4 (softcover)
      I. Title.
PS3521.L65T3   1991
811' .52--dc20   91-8593
                                   CIP

Published in 1991 by Sunstone Press
Post Office Box 2321
Santa Fe, New Mexico 87501

CONTENTS

The Taos Crescent

THE UPLIFT

Taos Valley is a huge amphitheater set in the crescent curve of soaring
       mountains, the skyline uplifting, inspiring what'er clear blue
       or storm dark thrilling in starlight mysteries in moonlight,
       the whole country magnetic, drawing various people
       through various centuries to it.
Who the first people to occupy Taos territory were is unknowable.
A roving proto-Ute stock seems to have developed the cliffcave
       pithouse, pueblo cultures.
Ethnologists postulate a Uto-Aztecan linguistic phylum which includes
       the Taos Tiwa language, Aztec Nahuatl, Paiute dialects, Hopi,
       Zuni, Pima, Papago, Comanche.
But it does not include the language of the Taos aborigines.
The word Taos was apparently first applied by Juan de Onate in 1598,
       derived from the Tewa word Ta-wii, meaning Dwell Gap.
Edward Curtis reports the Taos Indians called themselves Ta-i-na,
       meaning The People, or Ia-ta-i-na, meaning the
       Osier Willow People, probably referring to the red osier dogwood,
       Cornus stolonifera, the chewed bark of which abets fever,
       like quinine.
The real red willow is a salix species, the bark containing salycylic acid,
       aspirin.
The origin myth of the present Taos Indians asserts they emerged from
       a black lake up north, wandered many years, finally settled in
       the land of the red willows.
But their Tiwa language comes from the south, from the Piro Indians,
       a great people reputed to have once lived in an underground city,
       its location now lost.

The invasion of Spanish-speaking people begat miscegenation in
     Taos Tiwa-speaking people, and the English-speaking people
     begat interbreeding in both.
Linguistic distinctions are not racial distinctions.
There's no such thing as a fullblood Indian race, Spanish race,
     English race.
Moor, Jew, Greek, Scotch, Irish, Scandanvian, Navajo, Apache,
     Comanche components infuse the population of the Taos crescent.
The geologic distinctions are at least observable in the three
     classifications igneous, sedimentary, metamorphic.
North of the Indian pueblo canyon, igneous, plutonic formations prevail
     containing metal ores, copper, gold, scant silver.
South of the Indian canyon the formations are sedimentary,
     sandstones and limestones chiefly probably containing petroleum
     deep down.
And the south prong of the Taos crescent is metamorphic,
     containing alumininum silicates, staurolite crystals, garnets,
     kyanite, andalusite, adhesive clays.
The Rio Grande Gorge terminates the west end of the Taos crescent,
     a sheer-walled basaltic fissure.
It is a marvelous scenic setting, the natural beauty embracing
     abundant natural resources, and above all
     a feeling of livability.

ORIGIN MYTHS

All Indian origin myths are fantasies, none more so than the
    Biblical origin myth of Adam and Eve in the Garden of Eden.
Symbolically it is absurd and Freudian interpretations render it
    ugly and obscene.
The Male and female principals in Indian mythology are like
    yang and yin, never obscene but often jocose.
Modern scientists may win a booby prize with their chemico-genetic
    origin theories depicting an African Eve capable of
    self-reproduction
    the Mother of Mankind.
Human bones mixed with weird electronic instruments have been
    up in the proterozoic desert west of Pyramid Lake in Nevada,
    hence the origin of man was in America.
Land bridges and ice bridges across the Bering Straits and
    North Atlantic weren't necessary.
Eskimos roamed half way around the Arctic Circle.
Photosynthesis of primordial protoplasm seems the best starting point
    for Darwin's Origin of Species but he doesn't worry about it.
Nor could he discern in the course of evolution any general plan,
    purpose, design.
No teleology.
The Source of sources and end of ends were beyond speculation
    or deification.
There are concepts in his book, however, that apply today.
A great book, a masterpiece, along with Gray's Anatomy.

THE STRUGGLE FOR EXISTENCE

The anthropocentric attitude doesn't fit the strivings and struggles
    of non-human forms of life.
When fishermen failing to catch fish were told by Christ
    to cast their nets on the other side of the boat they did so and
    hauled in prodigious numbers of fish flipping and flopping on the
    bottom of the boat gasping for their element the water of the sea,
    gasping and gasping in agony till they died one by one.
Where was Christ's compassion?
    for the human stomach?
And the lone quail calling for its mate that hunters had shot,
    standing on a pile of rocks calling and calling,
    running to a seedy place pecking and scratching the ground
    to show her what to eat beside him but she never came,
    a pathetic little tragedy that haunted us with sadness.
Where was God's mercy?
    for the hungry hunter?
And the blasphemous infidel who was told by the Dominican Monk
    Tomas de Torquemada to believe in a merciful God
    or he would be pulled apart with stretcher, chains,
    Torquemada, the cruelist man in history, sadistically enjoying
    the screams of agony of his victims as their arms and legs
    were pulled apart.
The super-anthropocentric attitude, Torquemada abetted
    by the Borgia Pope, father of Lucretia.
Nay it goes all through nature.

THE IRRECONCILABLE INTERNECINE

Cat mauling a mouse, goshawk clutching a
    quail, piranhas ripping the flesh off a man,
    reducing him to a skeleton in a jiffy,
Man slaughtering animals, man slaughtering man,
    tribe against tribe, nation against nation,
    religion against religion, ideology against idelogy.
Holy Roman potentates put out the eyes of
    nightengales so they would sing blind,
    castrated choir boys so they would sing treble,
Coyotes kill cats and mice, sportsmen
    kill coyotes for their pelts and for a bounty,
Kill kill kill breed breed breed, perpetuate
    the strife of life, the irreconcilable internecine.
Jainists trample living things underfoot,
    vegetarians yank living plants out of
    the ground, crush cook eat.
The pitiless cosmos, existence consumed
    by existence, eon consumed by eon
    to what end, purpose, power, glory?
We cannot transcend, we can only confront, resolve, create.
Compassion is always there with the paradoxical pair
    good and evil, right and wrong, truth and beauty.

ESTHETIC JUDGEMENT

Esthetic judgement is the basic judgement
    of practical enterprise, the sense of
    beauty the ultimate evaluation.
Incentives, decisions, aspirations all are
    verbalities and all accede to the
    esthetic need.

RABBIT DANCE

The wellhouse was in a grassy glade in
    a gravelly mesa, chamisa and sage
    on the slanting slopes.
I was going to start the motor to pump
    water up to a tank in our house
    on a side mesa
But I stopped and crouched on my knees
    to watch the rarest performance I
    had ever seen in my life.
A rabbit dance! Hundreds of cottontail
    rabbits running at each other, leaping
    over each other, standing on their
    hind legs and touching their front
    paws together!
They didn't mind my presence, they were
    celebrating the joy of being alive,
    a pantheistic togetherness to it
    join our dance if you feel as we do.
About a month later at about the
    same time in the afternoon my
    wife and I were puzzled when our
    Indian friends Adam and Marie
    stopped at the glade and didn't come up to the house.
I went down to see what the trouble
    was. They were sitting in their
    car watching a rabbit dance!

Adam put his finger to his lips to warn
        me to approach quietly. I did and
        stood beside the car watching with them.
"They're like little people!" Marie
        whispered, and we watched till the
        rabbits suddenly whisked over the
        mesa and were gone.
Adam said neither he nor Marie had
        ever seen a rabbit dance before.
        The three of us consulted in old age
        that we never saw one again.

WHO OWNS THE LAND?

The oldtime Taos Indians claimed Pedernal Peak
    their boundary landmark west, Picuris Peak
    south, the mountains walling Eagle Nest Lake
    east, the ocher red cliffs of Questa north.
Spanish invaders claimed the country in the name
    of the Spanish king and Spanish God, divided
    it in land grants and family fincas, allotted
    the Taos Indians a tract of their own land
    and called it the Taos Pueblo Grant.
English-speaking settlers insisted on warranty
    deeds and patented titles but were never
    sure they really owned the land.
None of us owns it. We rent it. If we don't pay
    taxes the land is confiscated and sold to
    somebody else.
Ideally possession should be absolute,
    untaxable, untakeable, free dispensations,
    pay for description and recording and protection.
But government will confiscate government,
    politically insidious, war completer, and
    the stars tumble over the claims and controversies.

NICOLAS ROMERO

He farmed a finca strip of land, spoke
      pure Spanish, a beautiful language
      when enunciated clearly,
And he was genteel and courteous to friends
      and strangers alike, courteous to his
      land, treated it tenderly.
He felt the soil with his fingers, was it
      ready for ploughing and planting,
      irrigated it carefully the way he
      watered his stock.
His house was the largest in the district,
      a veritable hacienda, three sons, three
      sisters two of whom unmarried he took
      care of all their lives.
Agriculture is the basic culture, he contributed
      much to the economy of the country, meat
      and wheat, apples, pinto beans, chili.
The tentacles of religion didn't squeeze
      penances out of him, the church an agency
      registering birth, life, death God was a
      separate eminence rather than intimate
      emmanence.

RELLES

Born in the mountain meadowlands above
   Ocate, grass and shrub grazing for sheep
   and cattle, enough oak acorns edible raw,
Life was an epic from the beginning, and
   Relles worked hard, cheerfully, a fine spirit
   even as a little girl.
They traded wool for flour at Taos and Mora,
   a big church at Ocate alluring, a cozy
   wooden church near their ranch, country
   schoolteachers.
She married and settled in Taos near a
   Penitente morada, her husband belonged
   to the Brethren church, kindness instead
   of crucifixion.
He was a well-digger and wheat grower
   cut his crops by hand-sickle threshed
   it by hand, had it ground at the Taos
   steam-cylinder mill.
Four children, three sons, one daughter, Relles
   took work in town, scrubbed flooors,
   cleaned house, cooked Spanish dinners.
At home she chopped wood for the kitchen
   stove, cooked for the family, always cheerfully,
   a mother to neighbor children, fond of
   animals, two dogs, a horse.

We rented an old adobe house they had
      abandoned for a bigger home. It had
      an L-shaped courtyard shaded by
      a chokecherry tree and apricot tree.
We added a one-room studio to it at our
      own expense and added extra rent
      for it. They were desperately poor and
      a few extra dollars went a long way.
But Relles was rich in her knowledge of
      bygone days. She showed us how her
      grandmother carded wool, spun it by
      hand with distaff spindle, wove it.
She knew the oldtime medicines, Osha which
      cured about everything from common colds
      to pneumonia to stomachaches to heart
      trouble, an Immortal root, asclepias
      asperula, which she called Immortalis.
Her life was an epic, her love of life a lyric,
      the death of her son increasing her
      sharing the suffering of others her
      own death a loss to all who knew her.
She is buried in a local cemetery in the juniper foothills,
      a pathetic little headstone
      marking her grave, her soul greater
      than the soul of any pharoah buried
      in a golden coffin under a colossal pyramid.

THE ARTISTS

Bert Geer Phillips was the first settler. He married Doc
        Martin's sister and established a studio home across
        the road from the staunch country physician who
        mended everything from broken legs to bellyaches.
        Bert was a lifelong friend of the Taos Indians,
        painted them idyllic, a flute player, the moonlight song,
        man wooing maid in a wild iris meadow.
        His model Tol-du-la-pel-la, shortened Tolupela,
        Sun Lightning, helped him select the right subjects,
        interpreted ceremonial dances to him, but never
        reveled esoteric secrets. His special talent was
        color modulation whether with Indian backgrounds or
        autumn aspens, and facial modulations, as in his famous
        Mexican family picture. He was the first forest ranger
        in Taos, his rapport with nature substantial, and his
        rapport with the feelings of people was benign,
        a good artist, good man all the way through,
        he and his wife now buried side by side in the
        Sierra Vista cemetery of Taos.

Victor Higgins was the most introspective and self-critical
        of the Taos artists, questioned his subjects,
        questioned his style, questioned his motives,
        what was he trying to say? He sketched indoors and
        outdoors persistently, placement of objects,
        squareness and roundness, shades and lights,
        his classic Winter Funeral picture himself brooding
        over life and death.

Joseph Sharp was the camera copyist, his studio crammed
        with instruments to project a photogaph on canvas,
        trace it there with brush strokes, amend it with
        scrapes and erasers. Commissioned by Phoebe Hearst
        to do wild Indians he had to resort to the camera to
        record details, with no knowledge of meaning.
        He used the same magic lantern technique on the
        Taos Indians but he could and did paint intimate
        portraits direct and his landscape studies were
        free from mechanical contrivances. His life motive
        was obscure, no philosophy, no great masterpiece.

John Young-Hunter stylized his society portraits too slick,
        obtained a character essence in the very slickness,
        his study of Winston Churchill probing deep,
        he got the power of the man. His watercolor sketches
        were free and spontaneous, the bleakness or lushness
        of a landscape quick luminous clouds, you could hear
        the sage thrasher singing in the sagebrush.
        He was the only Taos artist who knew anything
        about birds, white-crowned sparrows, horned larks,
        chats, lazuli buntings, western evening grosbeaks,
        chewinks, kittyhawks, prairie falcons, eagles.
        He was not after fame of name. The Royal Academy
        established that. He was not after the money
        value of art. Bizarre subjects, bizarre techniques
        repelled him. Mabel Luhan was bizarre enough, his
        portrait of her subtly indicating the hard aquisitiveness
        of her eyes and mouth, she got what she wanted,
        an Indian husband or the necrophilic ashes of D.H. Lawrence
        in the shrine on the ranch she had given him.

Ken Adams was the one artist who didn't kowtow to her.
Don't let her get you into her clutches, he said,
she'll take your scalp and nail it on the wall as a trophy.
Ken kowtowed to the Great Master Andrew Dasburg
who kowtowed to Mabel but shook off his prestige
and painted unformula flower studies and portraits.
His picture of his first wife Hilda is a museum piece,
the phases of feeling of a T.B. hypochondriac, the
color nuances, the greenish haze. The Hondo Canyon
was his favorite sketching ground, wild cliffs,
wildflowers, blue columbine, fringed gentian,
rushing stream, old mine and when the ski lodge people
took it over he said I'll never come here again.
He taught art at the University, married a very
understanding and charming second wife after
Hilda died, painted still life flower studies,
kept his Taos friends, spoofed the artists.

Oscar Berninghaus was noted for his "Peace and Plenty"
        picture, an old Indian standing in a sparse room
        contented with the colored Indian corn, pile of squash,
        and conjugal domesticity of his wife seated on a bench
        handling a basket of food, and his painting of unseen
        cowboys in a saloon on a cold winter night was famous,
        the lamp light from the single window showing their
        horses tethered to a hitching rail outside in the snow.
        "He handles crowds well," Ken Adams observed,
        the one of a fiesta crowd on a hot summer day palpable,
        the individual faces of those seeking shade under a
        giant cottonwood, others sweltering, you could see
        and feel the heat waves shimmering in the air.
        "I'm just a painter of pictures," said Berny.
        "I'm not a great genius promoting myself like Blumy."

Blumenschein, Ernest L. Blumenschein, Blumy, proclaimed
    himself the greatest artist in Taos therefore the
    greatest in America, and he did elicit a dynamic
    essence with his chunky clumpy hills, pancake clouds,
    umbrella trees, a more powerful effect with the
    basaltic blocks of his canyon pictures. His arrogant
    conceit was balanced by an abject humility, he
    overworked his paintings, erased a spot with solvents,
    repainted it while still wet, the thick pigments often
    cracking. He had been a virtuoso violinist till he
    injured the fingers of his left hand, he was an expert
    bridge player and tennis player, he jumped from one
    thing to another. "He has the mind of a flea and the
    soul of a gnat," said Walter Ufer. His masterpiece is an
    illustration titled "Superstition," a man lying on his
    back on a couch, eyes credulous, mouth open,
    tongue tasting his fatuous beliefs, a miniature group of
    Indians painted on his belt indulging their superstition
    dancing for rain.

Irving Couse walking to town with his hands behind his back,
    walking home to his beautiful studio and oriental
    poppies on a hillside was a familiar and likeable Taos
    figure. His commissioned works, Indians squatting
    by a hearth fire, Indians with flutes and drums in
    various poses, had a reality of their own and his larger
    museum canvases are historical.

Martin Hennings and Herbert "Buck" Duntion were horse lovers
    as well as landscape lovers, their work excellent
    technically and expressively.

Walter Ufer's profanity spiced conversations, his work
        not up to his own standards, he knew it was hollow,
        blasphemed Government projects.

Georgia O'Keeffe tried Taos out, rented a glass gazebo room
        atop the Chamisal Lodge, moved to Ghost Ranch,
        moved to Abiquiu.
        "Her preoccupation with genitalia is disgusting,"
        said Mabel Luhan, and Mabel ought to know.

The impact of the first wave of Taos artists didn't erode
the subject matter too much and the second wave
constisted of more versatile attitudes, Emil Bisttram
with his dynamic symmetry abstractions,
Thomas Benrimo with his Salvador Dali extensions,
Ward Lockwood, Carl Woolsey, Wood Woolsey,
the etchers Howard Cook, Doel Reed, Gene Kloss,
the woodcarvers Max Luna, Pat Barela, Gustave
Hildebrand, portraits by Nichlai Fechin, Ila McAfee's
horse patterns, Elmer Turner's concise contours
and colors, Joseph Imhof's limestone lithographs,
Barbara Latham's humorous woodcuts, and her
galloping rabbit-hunt oils, Duane Van Vechten's
individualistic abstractions, Helen Blumenschein's
excellent unadvertised portraits. The third wave of
Taos artists is still splashing.

HEE-LEE-WA-WA

Hee-lee-wa-wa, Indians say,
All gone, what will stay?
Sweet nostalgic memories
Our own end puts an end to these.
Nothing abides, Lucretius said,
Not even the deadness of the dead
Dissolved in the dust of eternity's span
Nary a whisper where once was a man;
Eternity likewise a mere verbality
Perishing with infinity in unreality,
Time-space words we vainly construe
And set a place for heaven too.
The diction we need is how can we hold
Economic development from overload,
Confront it in poetry, confront it in prose,
Save the wild bird, save the wild rose
In rhythm and rhyme written forced and fondly
Iambic, paeonic, anapest, spondee.
We need not become like Las Vegas, Nevada,
The meaning of life nada y nada.
Just jet planes and booze and sex and sin
Traffic jams and din and din.
Hee-lee-wa-wa the joy of the meadowlark's song
And linnets and birds that used to belong
Hee-lee-wa-wa the very stars at night

Blazed out of sight by a beacon light
Hee-lee-wa-wa the quail call and sound of doves
And lost little creatures with lost little loves.
Tsanoff countered it best, I think,
He felt the uplift and saw the sink
Quoted Kant and Croce, Sinclair lewis
Ibsen's Master Builder and Lady From the Sea
Esthetics conjoined mystically.
Moses on the mountain in the lightning and
        the thunder
Found the Ten Commandments on a tablet
        carved thereunder
Morality more than rules of conduct,
        Tsanoff noted, defined it deeper.
He was one of the great minds drawn
        to Taos, Tsanoff,
But couldn't analyze the draw,
His wife reflective, convective, and
        as likeable as he,
Her quest a house in Taos.
Brett built one near Lawrence's shrine
And named it after Jeffer's poem
The Tower Beyond Tragedy.
She was deaf and thrust her
        ear trumpet Toby at you.
"It looks like rain today," I teased
"That is not a very original remark,"
        she rebuked in her British accent.

She painted Stokowski's hands
        conducting a concert, not able
        to hear the sounds.
He rejected her interest in him, took
        a notion to Greta Garbo till
        Gloria Vanderbuilt got him.
Brett wrote a book titled "Lawrence
        and Brett: A Friendship."
Spud Johnson corrected spelling and
        grammar, the actual ghost writer for her.

She painted a picture of Taos Indian women dancing the
        Circle Dance, brightened the colors of the costumes,
        sketched the background with slight realistic strokes.
        She moved from her Tower Beyond Tragedy
        to a more convenient location nearer town,
        painted eccentric pictures, wore eccentric clothes,
        English riding britches with leather puttees,
        an embroidered vest, cowboy shirt with a flaring tie,
        cowboy hat. As a Taos character she took her place
        with Long John Dunn Doughbelly Price, Cap O'Hay,
        Mabel Luhan, Doc Martin, Gertrude Light,
        Mike Cunico, Bertha Gusdorf, Anastacio Santistevan.

Hee-lee-wa-wa eventually to all things great and small.
    Nothing abides says lucretius, Beethoven's
    Appassionata Seventeeth Sonata, Sixteenth quartet.
    Verdi, Donizetti, Puccini, Berlioz's Lachrymose.
    Tschaikovsky's Sixth Symphony.
    Michael Faraday's physics. The Faraday Cage
    anticipating Einstein's relativity.
    Frames of reference. Hee-lee-wa-wa
    the very concepts Hee-lee-wa-wa the beauty of life
    that makes life worth living.
    Then what? And whatness is a verbality.

STAUROLITE

Staurolite crystals in micaceous schist
Twinned at ninety or sixty degree
Crosses and x's, single in slate
Iron aluminum silicate.
Eroded from the matrix clean-cut crosses make
Solid little crucifixes pendants for a necklace,
Small ones set in silver rings
The vanity of holy things.
Lagrimas de Cristo or Lucky stones they're called
Hidden or exposed in the southern hills of Taos.
Myriad forms of thought the incandescent mind takes
Potential design in the seed of a flower
Rainbow refracting the shine or shower
Whatever the form in snow, schist, or slate
There is no prefixed form of fate.

ABOUT THE AUTHOR

Phillips Kloss was born in Webster Groves, Missouri in 1902.
His first aquaintance with New Mexico came in 1916 when
he worked on his brother's ranch. In 1925 he graduated from
the University of California at Berkeley. Two years later
he was back in New Mexico, this time with his wife,
Alice Geneva Glasier (Gene Kloss). In the years that followed,
living both in New Mexico and on the coast of California,
Mr. Kloss established himself nationally as an important poet
and critic. Today, Phillips and Gene Kloss live and work in
Taos, New Mexico. In addition to this volume, Sunstone Press has
published *The Great Kiva, Gene Kloss Etchings, Selected Poems of
Phillips Kloss* and *Rainbow Obsidian.*

www.ingramcontent.com/pod-product-compliance
Lightning Source LLC
Chambersburg PA
CBHW031153090426
42738CB00008B/1311